Marvelous Grace

24 Gospel Songs
Arranged for Ladies' Voices

by Mosie Lister

Lillenas PUBLISHING COMPANY

Kansas City, MO 64141

Contents

Canaanland Is Just in Sight

Words and Music by
JEFF GIBSON
Arranged by Mosie Lister

9

He's Still the King of Kings

WILLIAM J. GAITHER, and
GLORIA GAITHER

WILLIAM J. GAITHER
Arranged by Mosie Lister

sound of the trum-pet, the skies blaze with fire; Moun-tains

thun - der with God's judg - ment ring - ing;

Divisi

But the saints have no fear their Re -

deem - er has come, "Praise the Lord," thro' all

16

Grace

with

Grace Greater than Our Sin

Words and Music by
PAMELA FURR, WAYNE HAUN
and RAYMOND C. DAVIS
Arranged by Marty Parks
S.S.A. Arrangement by Mosie Lister

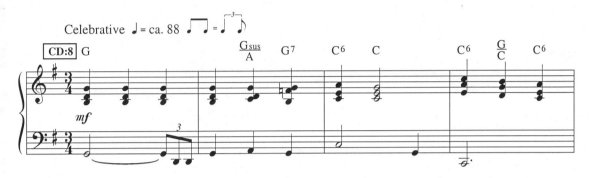

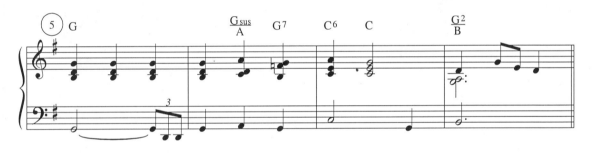

*Track includes string pad as guide. Track may be stopped on beat 3 of measure 104 if guide is not desired or needed.

All of Me

[S.S.A.(A)]
A cappella

Words and Music by
MOSIE LISTER
Arranged by Mosie Lister

Worshipful ♩ = ca. 80

All of me, Not a part, but all of me, All the heart and

soul of me, Je-sus, I sur-ren-der. Oo_____

All_____ of me, Thro' the a-ges yet to be, I sur-ren-der,

Lord, to Thee; I sur-ren-der all of me, all of me.

I sur-ren-der_____ all, all_____ of me._____

New Shoes

Words and Music by
MOSIE LISTER
Arranged by Mosie Lister

tell the world___ that Je - sus saves.___

I'll go where He leads___ me,___ wher -

ev - er that may be, And I'll tell the world___ that

CD: 14

Solo

Je - sus saves. The Book says

Love Was in the Room

KEN BIBLE and
MOSIE LISTER

MOSIE LISTER
Arranged by Mosie Lister

broke thro' to the dark-ness of the tomb,
broke thro' to the dark-ness of my tomb,

C   F

(17)

And the love of the Fa-ther came and
And the love of the Fa-ther came and

F   G

CD: 18 1st time
CD: 20 2nd time

filled ev-ery cor-ner of that room.
filled ev-ery cor-ner of my room.

Dm⁷   G⁶ G F/G G⁷   C

Jesus, the Son of God

KEN BIBLE and
G. T. HAYWOOD

G. T. HAYWOOD
Arranged by Mosie Lister

That Says It All

Words and Music by
MOSIE LISTER
Arranged by Mosie Lister

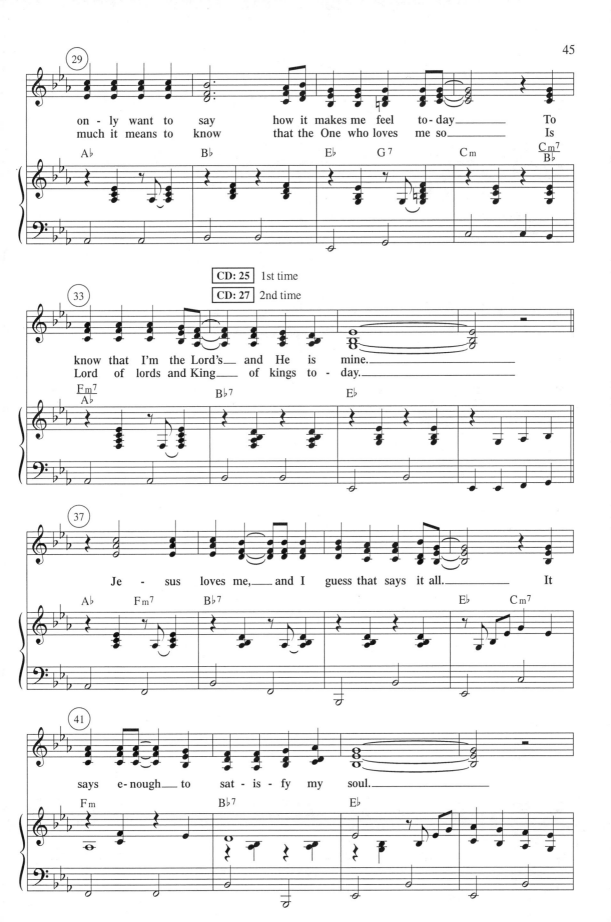

(to pg. 43, meas. 1)

Beyond the Cross

Words and Music by
MOSIE LISTER
Arranged by Mosie Lister

52

O Lord, How Wonderful

[S.S.A.(A)]
A cappella

MOSIE LISTER and
KEN BIBLE

MOSIE LISTER
Arranged by Mosie Lister

Well Done, My Child

Words and Music by
TONY WOOD and DANNY MYRICK
Arranged by Richard Kingsmore
S. S. A. Arrangement by Mosie Lister

Unison

③⑨

wait - ing._____ Here is your robe of white, your man - sion is just in sight, come in - to this cit - y of light,_____ Well done, my child."

④③

CD: 35

④⑦

Solo **mf**

When I

His Hand in Mine

Words and Music by
MOSIE LISTER
Arranged by Mosie Lister

step I take, and if I fall,_____ I know He'll un - der -

stand. Till the day He tells me why_____ He loves me

so,_____ I can feel His hand in mine; that's

all I need to know._____ I can feel His

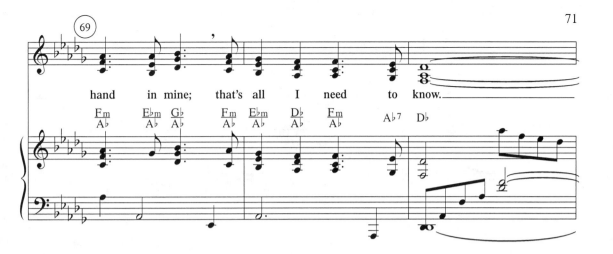

hand in mine; that's all I need to know.

I can feel His hand in mine; that's all I

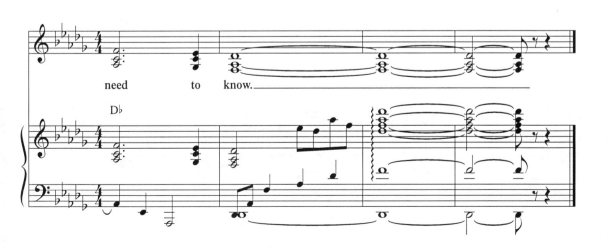

need to know.

Keep on the Firing Line

Unknown
Arranged by Mosie Lister

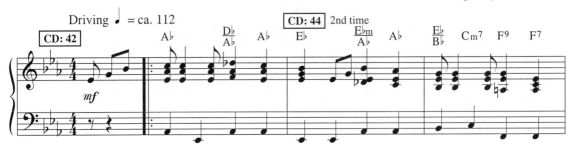

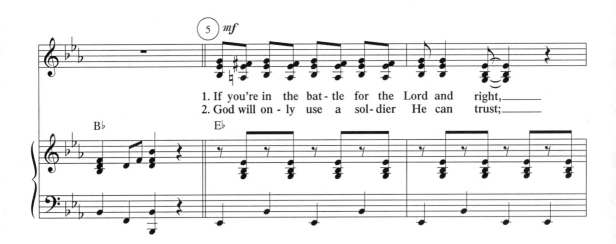

1. If you're in the bat-tle for the Lord and right,_____
2. God will on-ly use a sol-dier He can trust;_____

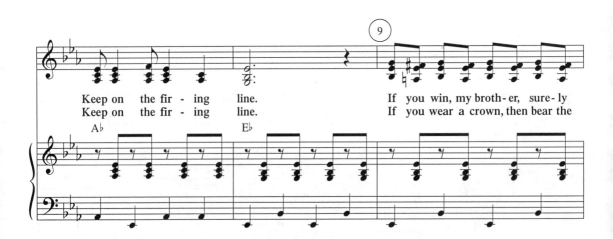

Keep on the fir - ing line.
Keep on the fir - ing line.

If you win, my broth-er, sure-ly
If you wear a crown, then bear the

74

Lead - ing them to Je - sus from the paths of sin,_____

CD: 46

With a shout of wel - come we will all march in,_____ So_____

keep on the fir - ing line. O you must

fight, be brave a - gainst all e - vil, Nev - er run_____ nor

The Night Before Easter

Words and Music by
DONNIE SUMNER
and DWAYNE FRIEND
Arranged by Mosie Lister

44 mo - ment lies___ si - lent and still.

Eb7 Ab

48 *Divisi* But a Pow - er sent from heav - en comes___

Eb Ab Ab7/C

52 break - ing the night, And___ death must___

Bbm/Db Db Bbm7 Eb7 Db/Eb

CD: 52 *Unison* bow to His will. Then a

Eb7 Db/Eb Eb7 Ab

Call Home

Words and Music by
MOSIE LISTER
Arranged by Mosie Lister

There is a mo - ment that lives for - ev - er;

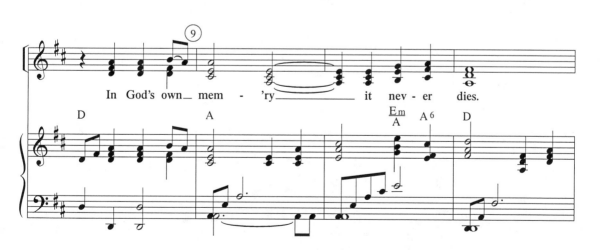

In God's own mem - 'ry it nev - er dies.

Lay These Burdens Down

[S.S.A.(A)]
A cappella

Words and Music by
MOSIE LISTER
Arranged by Mosie Lister

With Anticipation ♩ = ca. 104

1. Been trav-'ling this road so long now, But I'll keep mov-ing a-
(2. This) jour-ney will soon be o - ver; This night will soon___ be

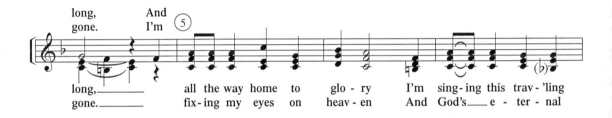

long, And I'm
gone.

long,___ all the way home to glo - ry I'm sing-ing this trav-'ling
gone.___ fix-ing my eyes on heav - en And God's___ e - ter - nal

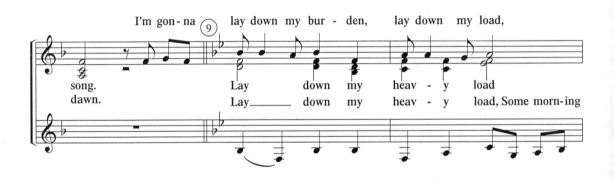

I'm gon - na lay down my bur - den, lay down my load,

song. Lay down my heav - y load
dawn. Lay___ down my heav - y load, Some morn-ing

Lay down my cares at the end of the road. Sing "Hal - le - lu - jah,"

When ends this long, long road. Sing O so
when shall end this long, long road. And I will sing___ O so

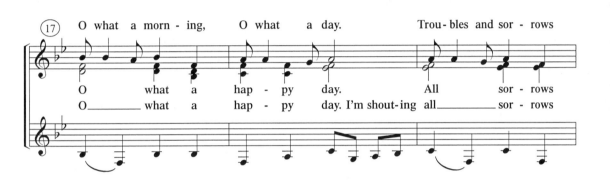

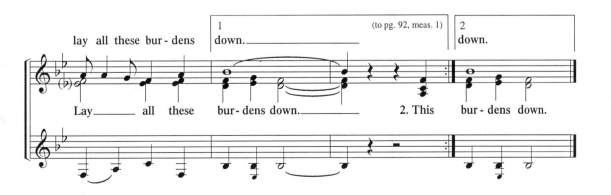

Wedding Music

with
Celebrate His Coming

Words and Music by
KIRK TALLEY and PHIL CROSS
Arranged by Tom Fettke
S.S.A. Arrangement by Mosie Lister

bride's a-dorned and read - y to ap - pear.

There's heav-en-ly prep - a - ra - tion For the

wed-ding cel - e - bra - tion. Is that wed - ding

mu - sic that I hear?

CD: 61

*"Celebrate His Coming"

The Light from Heaven

Words and Music by
MOSIE LISTER
Arranged by Mosie Lister

The Man on the Middle Cross

Words and Music by
MOSIE LISTER
Arranged by Mosie Lister

I'm Not Giving Up

Words and Music by
SQUIRE E. PARSONS, JR.
Arranged by Mosie Lister

Here Comes the King

MOSIE LISTER
and KEN BIBLE

MOSIE LISTER
Arranged by Mosie Lister

Thro'-out all cre-a-tion ex-cite-ment is

ris-ing. God's gath-ered peo-ple are start-ing to

CD: 80

In the Name of Love

Words and Music by
MOSIE LISTER
Arranged by Mosie Lister

124